MUSEUM SERIES

Ancient
China

Written by

Diane Sylvester

Illustrated by

Corbin Hillam

2006 • THE LEARNING WORKS

The Learning Works

Editor: Pam VanBlaricum
Illustrator: Corbin Hillam
Text Design: Acorn Studio Books
Cover Designer: Barbara Peterson
Cover Illustration: Gary Ciccarelli
Project Director: Linda Schwartz

Contents

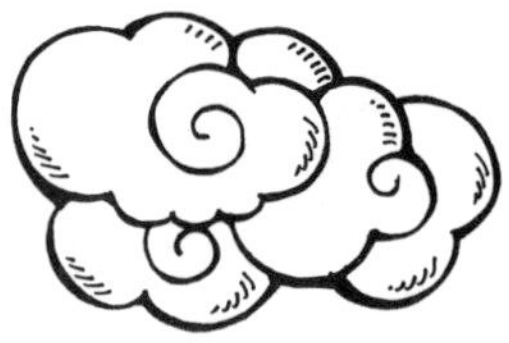

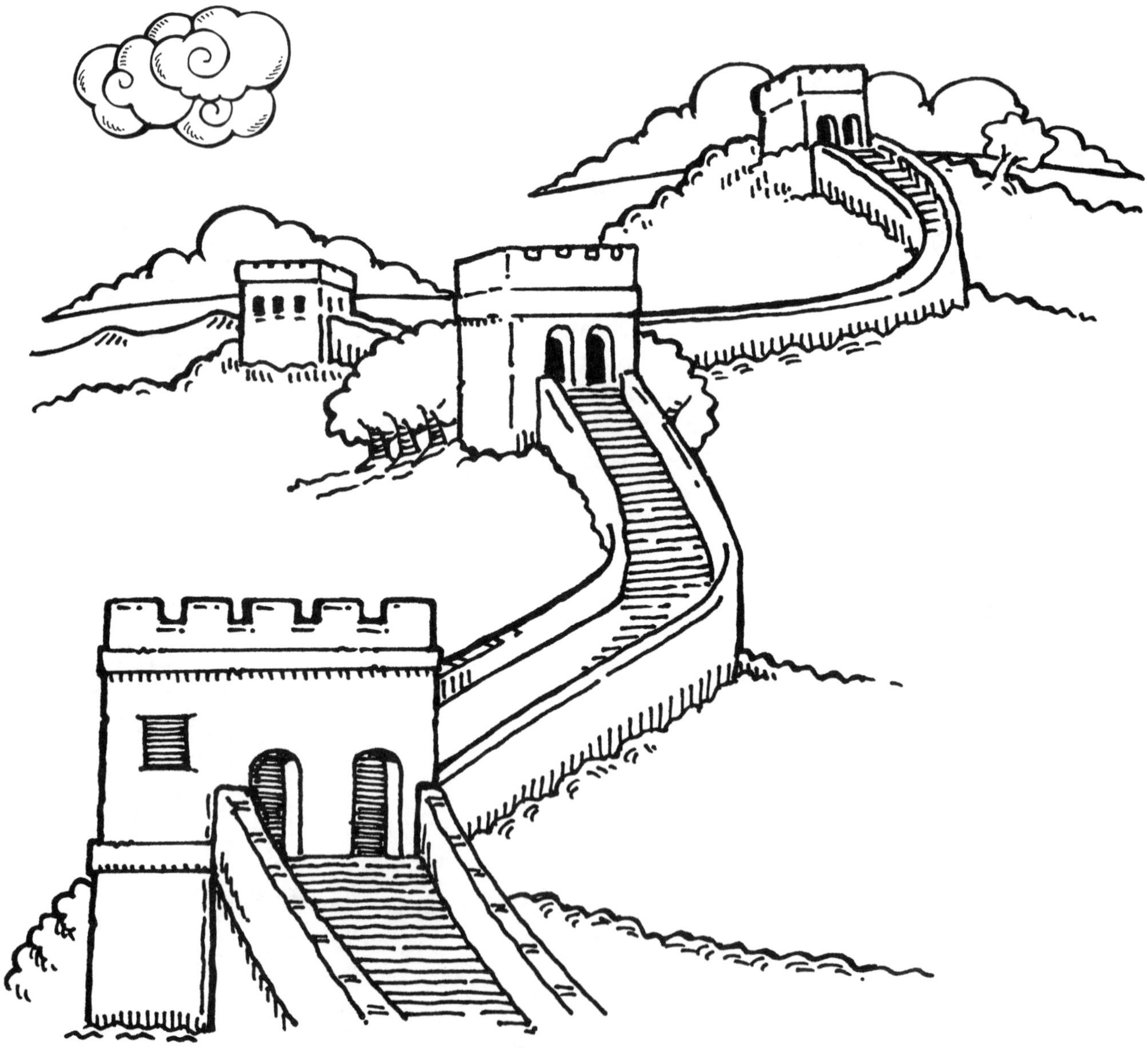

To the Teacher

Purpose

Museums are storehouses of interesting things that help us learn more about our natural and physical world. The purpose of this book is to provide ideas and activities to help students create their own amazing museum full of specially crafted artifacts from the ancient civilization of China.

The projects and activities in this book highlight the economic, political, social, scientific, and cultural components upon which all civilizations are based.

The projects and activities also provide opportunities for students to

- plan and give oral presentations
- plan and conduct guided tours
- plan and create graphs, labels, and posters
- refine map reading skills

Social Studies Standards

The content of this book meets the following social studies standards:

Understand the geographic features that influenced China's growth and history.

Learn about Confucius and Buddha.

Learn about the policies and achievements of the emperor Qin Shi Huang.

Learn about the significance of the Silk Road.

Make and use maps and charts to analyze location.

Describe the role of technology in shaping the characteristics of China.

Describe the impact of trade and transportation on the spread of ancient China.

Understand the religious traditions and how they shaped ancient Chinese culture.

Learn about the cultural and scientific contributions of ancient China.

Tips and Ideas for Setting Up the Ancient China Museum

Creating a museum is often used as a culmination to a unit of study. However, creating a museum can be a unit by itself—full of educational and motivational activities and projects. The following ideas will help you set up your ancient civilization museum.

Decisions to make before you begin

Where will the museum be located?

What roles will students assume in creating the artifacts and in displaying them?

How many artifacts will be included in the museum?

How will the students be grouped for each activity (individual, small group, or entire class)?

Although it is obvious that the students are making replicas, models, and designs of artifacts, a decision needs to be made whether they will be referred to as real objects in the museum or as student-built and designed displays.

Suggestions for student roles

(The teacher should decide whether or not to assume the roles of Museum Director and/or Curator)

Museum Director: this person assigns roles; coordinates lessons and activities

Curator: this person chooses the artifacts to be constructed and displayed; oversees placement of artifacts in museum; oversees labeling and educational material accompanying artifact

Design and Planning Specialists: students, or small groups of students, plan, make, and display artifacts

Public Education Advisors: students write scripts for tours; oversee training tour guides; and create advertising or educational videos

Advertisers: students create brochures, posters, advertisements, and invitations

Reporters: students write articles for class newspaper or other school publications

Tour Guides: students lead parents and other students on tour of museum

Tips and Ideas for Setting Up
the Ancient China Museum *(continued)*

Suggestions for planning and creating your museum

Give your museum a creative name.

Make a large map of China.

Make a mural highlighting important achievements in various Chinese dynasties.

Consider making artifacts in a variety of ways—drawn, sculpted, carved, modeled, sewn, photographed, etc.

Consider using a variety of materials for the artifacts such as clay, papier mache, cardboard, wood, yarn, foil, etc.

The exhibit displays can be set on stands, put in boxes, hung from ceilings, attached to walls, placed on floors, etc.

Make signs for museum—posters, bulletin boards, display stands, etc.

Publicize exhibit by creating pamphlets, posters, brochures, advertisements, videos, etc.

Create tour brochures, tour guide speeches, and audio tours.

Invite other classes and parents to the Grand Opening of museum.

The Grand Opening of the museum can begin with a Chinese parade led by students carrying dragon masks. Other students can play cymbals, triangles, sticks, and drums. In addition, students can dress appropriately to represent emperors, poets, historical figures, and common folk.

Invitation to the Grand Opening
of the Ancient China Museum

cut here

- -

Celebrate the Grand Opening of the

ꡖ Ancient China Museum ꡖ

Date: _____   Time: _____

Location: _____

_____

Organized and Created by

_____

_____

_____

Exhibits • Displays • Ancient Artifacts • Personal Tours

- -

cut here

Exhibit Description Card

Directions

Photocopy exhibit cards on heavyweight paper. Make one card per exhibit. Complete the information, fold the card, and place it alongside the museum artifact.

fold here

🔳 Ancient China Museum 🔳

Name of artifact: _____

Description: _____

_____

_____

_____

Designed and created by _____

Ancient China Project Proposal

Directions

Submit a completed *Ancient China Project Proposal* to your Museum Director or Curator for approval.

Name(s): _____

Title of artifact/project: _____

Description of artifact/project: _____

_____

_____

What materials will you need? _____

_____

_____

How much room in the museum will your project need? _____

Write a short script describing the artifact/project for a museum tour guide to use:

_____

_____

_____

_____

_____

Ancient China © 2006 The Learning Works

Brochure for the Grand Opening
of the Ancient China Museum

Directions

Design a brochure or flyer that describes the exhibits in your museum. You may use the art on this page or draw your own illustrations.

Ancient China © 2006 The Learning Works

China—The World's Oldest Empire

Chinese civilization, the world's oldest still in existence, has a recorded history dating back more than 3,500 years. For much of its long history, China remained a world unto itself, isolated by hundreds of rivers, impassable mountains, hostile deserts, and vast steppes. As a result, the Chinese came to regard their country as the center of the civilized world and called their homeland Zhong Guo, or Middle Kingdom.

Project Description

Use a piece of poster board to make a map of China which includes major rivers, lakes, mountains, deserts, and seas, and shows historical cities of China. Draw in and label the Great Wall, Valley of the Ming Tombs, the Grand Canal, the Silk Road, the site of the Terra Cotta Warriors, and other places pertinent to the artifacts in the museum. Display the map in a prominent location in the museum.

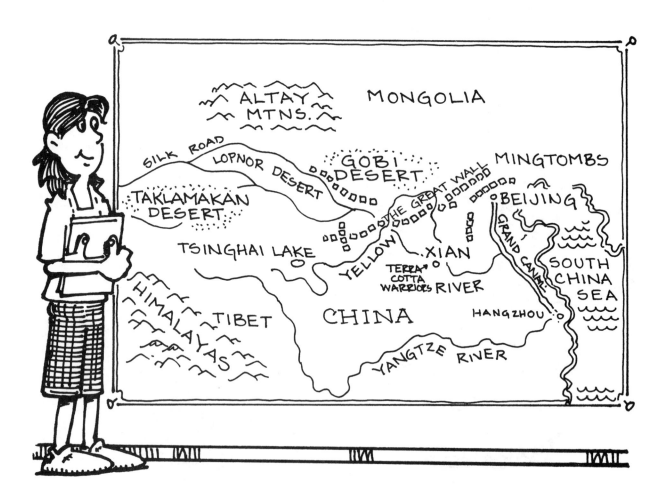

Important Chinese Dynasties

Chinese history is marked by a cycle of power struggles, each started by a military leader determined to create a unified nation. Each leader created a dynasty by naming himself emperor and passing the leadership on to his eldest son. Some Chinese dynasties endured for more than three centuries; others were much shorter.

Highlights of Important Chinese Dynasties

Xia Dynasty, 2100–1600 B.C.
Silk production begins

Shang Dynasty, 1600–1100 B.C.
Chariots used in warfare; advanced writing system in use

Zhou Dynasty, 1100–221 B.C.
Iron casting and multiplication tables invented

Qin Dynasty, 221–206 B.C.
Great Wall completed; writing system, money, weights and measures, and cart axle length are standardized

Han Dynasty, 206 B.C.– 220 A.D.
Paper is invented; eclipses predicted; steel is manufactured; first national library established

Tang Dynasty, 618–907
Age of poetry is founded; figure painting and landscape art flourish; porcelain and gunpowder are invented

Song Dynasty, 960–1279
Genghis Khan is emperor; Mongols conquer north China

Yuan (Mongol) Dynasty, 1271–1368
Kublai Khan rules; Marco Polo travels in China; drama flourishes

Ming Dynasty, 1368–1644
Great Wall is extended; naval expeditions sent to Indian Ocean and Africa

Qing Dynasty (or Manchu), 1644–1912
Foreigners dominate China; the last emperor rules

Project Description

When you write the description card for the items that will be in your museum, try to identify the dynasty in which it was invented, built, or gained popularity.

Terra Cotta Statues

According to an old Chinese legend, the first emperor of China, Qin Shi Huang (259 B.C.–210 B.C.) was born with the nose of a scorpion, the eyes of a vulture, the heart of a tiger, and the voice of a wolf. He purportedly killed thousands of scholars and burned the books of philosophers whose views differed from his. But he was also responsible for unifying China by standardizing the written language, the system of weights and measures, and the shapes and sizes of money. This allowed people who spoke different languages to trade and communicate with one another.

Qin Shi Huang planned an elaborate burial complex for his eventual death. Nearly 700,000 workers spent thirty-six years constructing more than 6,000 life-size terra cotta warriors, including officers, cavalrymen with horses, and charioteers with full fighting gear. Each soldier wore the uniform of his rank and had individualized facial features, height, and hairstyle. The clay soldiers were placed underground and a wooden roof was built over them and covered with soil. The terra cotta army lay undisturbed until 1973 when it was accidentally discovered by a peasant drilling a well. Qin Shi Huang's tomb continues to be extensively excavated.

Terra Cotta Statues *(continued)*

Project Description

Imagine that you are working alongside archaeologists at Qin Shi Huang's tomb. They are excavating artifacts of soldiers, horses, and chariots. Study the warriors and determine which one should be represented in the Ancient China Museum. Make a clay model of it.

Materials

Clay or sculpting materials that don't require firing or
baking. Several types dry bone hard and can be
decorated, painted, and modified by sanding or filing.

Tools for sculpting:
toothpicks
paring knife or utility blade
coffee stirrers
cuticle sticks
textures from fabrics, window screen, sandpaper,
emery boards
plastic forks and knives
craft sticks
grater for making hair

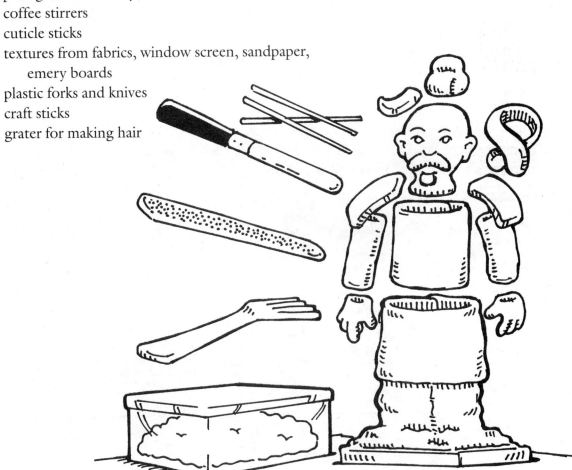

Ancient China © 2006 The Learning Works

Terra Cotta Statues *(continued)*

Directions

1. Decide on the size and type of terra cotta artifact you will sculpt. You'll probably need 1–2 pounds clay for each figure. Store extra clay in a sealable plastic bag or in a container with a lid. With air-dry clay, it is important to cover it with a wet cloth when not working on it.

2. Keep your sculpture on a piece of board or thick paper while working on it. Use the pinch method to anchor the feet to the base. Make it solid for stability.

3. Begin by rolling a slab into a tube-shape to form the body.

4. Add arms, hands, and head. Hints: Roll a piece of clay into a ball to make the warrior's head. Roll out clay "worms" for legs and arms. Push a piece of clay through a cheese grater to make hair.

5. Add details by using some of the tools suggested on page 15.

6. When originally created, the terra cotta figures were fully painted. Time and exposure to the elements have stripped away most of the paint. Keep your figure in its original clay color, or paint it realistically.

7. When originally created, the warriors were armed with bronze weapons such as swords, daggers, spears, axes, and crossbows. Over 10,000 bronze weapons have been excavated from the site. Create weapons out of clay, or make them out of paper, foil, sticks, etc.

 Ancient China © 2006 The Learning Works

The Great Wall

The Great Wall is the longest structure ever built. It stretches for nearly 4,000 miles from the Yellow Sea through the mountains and deserts of China. The oldest portions of the wall can be traced back to about the 400s B.C. At that time, feudal kingdoms built walls around their territories as protection against invasion by nomadic tribes in the north. These original walls were eventually joined into one long barrier under the leadership of Qin Shi Huang.

The wall itself was never a complete barrier to invasion, but it did remind invaders of China's military strength. The wall's effectiveness depended on efficient communication between the watchtowers and a well-run military organization. The wall gave China a definite border and defined the country. Today it is a symbol of the longevity of the Chinese empire and continues to be the most popular tourist site in China.

Ancient China © 2006 The Learning Works

The Great Wall *(continued)*

Project Description

Create a portion of the Great Wall that would astound Qin Shi Huang in its creativity and ability to protect his empire. Place your model in the Ancient China Museum.

Guidelines for Building a Model Section

1. If the wall is built in sections, standardize the dimensions so the sections fit together.

2. Include several major components—gates, signal towers or beacons, moats, and walls.

3. Build a gate to allow controlled entry to and from China. Gates can vary from a simple double wall to a virtual castle with a maze-like passage to the other side of the wall.

4. Build walls that allow room for both horses and men. Include ramps and ladders to allow men and horses to access the top of the wall.

5. Communication between the army units was important. During daylight hours, smoke signals were widely used. At night, lanterns and beacon fires were used. Other means of signaling included the use of flags, clappers, drums, and bells. Build a signal tower.

6. Builders of the wall made good use of natural features which accounts for the dragon-like appearance of the Great Wall as it winds its way across China. Try to make your model look authentic by having it wind up and down several hills.

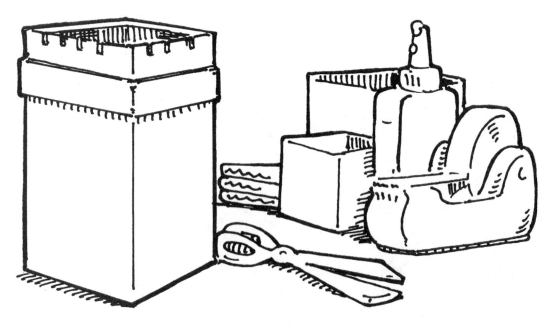

Ancient China © 2006 The Learning Works

The Great Wall *(continued)*

Materials

cardboard, poster board, or boxes of various sizes
scissors
masking tape
glue
other types of paper that will add to the overall authenticity
paint, markers

Directions

1. Decide on the dimensions of your section of the Great Wall. Make a template for the height and width at the top of the walls. Take into account that eight horses often rode side by side on the walls.

2. First design your section of the wall on paper. Follow the guildlines on the preceding page.

3. Draw and cut out your paper patterns.

4. Trace your patterns onto cardboard and cut them out.

5. Assemble the cardboard pieces using tape and glue.

6. Decorate the wall with paints, markers, other paper, or other items to make it look authentic.

 Ancient China © 2006 The Learning Works

Chinese Dragons

If you imagine a dragon as being fierce and fire-breathing and pursued by knights in armor, then your image differs from the Chinese version of a dragon. Chinese dragons may be wild and temperamental, but they are never evil. In fact, they are thought to bring good luck. Chinese dragons come in many different colors, sizes, and shapes; they have the ability to change size or shape; and they are even able to disappear into pools, lakes, oceans, and clouds. According to Chinese mythology, the dragon is coaxed from its lair during the new year by a dazzling red pearl and the loud sounds of cymbals, drums, gongs, and firecrackers. A five-clawed dragon is a symbol of the emperor and is found carved on royal thrones and embroidered on silk robes.

Chinese Dragons *(continued)*

Project Description

Pretend that you are visiting a famous museum of antiquities. A mysterious crate is delivered and when it is opened, you realize immediately that you are looking at a dragon mask that was probably used in a new year celebration for an ancient Chinese emperor. Use papier mache to replicate this dragon mask so it can be placed in your Ancient China Museum.

Materials

Papier mache projects are made from a paper pulp, a shaped form, and paste. Projects are easy to make—basically layering of paper over a shape—but can be messy and take several days to dry. Instant papier mache products are available from craft stores.

Pulp: Newspaper is a key ingredient for the papier mache pulp. Newspaper can also be used for creating details such as horns, claws, and eyes. Other types of papers can be used, too, such as paper towels, tissue paper, and toilet paper. Some people recommend using brown paper bags because they are cleaner to work with. Interesting effects can be achieved with fancy wrapping papers.

Paste: There are many different recipes for papier mache paste although the easiest is either liquid starch or a mixture of one part water with two parts white glue.

Materials to use for the dragon form:
toilet paper and paper towel rolls
egg cartons
paper cups
cardboard boxes such as cereal boxes and shoe boxes
crumpled or rolled newspapers
crunched aluminum foil

Other materials:
masking tape for holding the form components together
bowl for paste
scissors
brushes to brush on paste, if preferred
tempera or poster paints
decorating items such as crepe paper, ribbons, glitter, beads, yarn, etc.

Chinese Dragons *(continued)*

Directions

1. Design a dragon head on paper and then create the form out of suggested materials on the preceding page.

2. Tear or cut paper into strips.

3. Pour paste into a bowl. Dip each strip into the paste a few seconds, but don't leave it long; you want it sticky, not soaked. You can also use a brush to apply the paste.

4. Place the strip where you want it on the form and smooth it down. Let the first layer dry thoroughly before adding another layer. It will also work to apply three or four layers before letting it dry, especially if time is short.

5. Use crushed or rolled newspaper to make horns, eyes, nose, or teeth. Use masking tape to attach these and other appendages to the form. Papier mache the appendages.

6. Apply a final layer of white paper (paper towels, white tissue paper) so that the paint goes on easier.

7. Let the mask dry completely, and then paint it in traditional Chinese patterns.

8. When the paint has dried, decorate the mask with decorative and dramatic items.

Ancient China © 2006 The Learning Works

Chinese Lanterns

The Lantern Festival is a traditional Chinese festival started in the Han Dynasty (206 B.C.–220 A.D.), and held on the 15th day of the first lunar month of the Chinese new year. On the night of the festival, with a full moon shining brightly in the sky, people go into the streets carrying a variety of lanterns, watch dragons dancing, play games, and set off firecrackers.

Chinese Lanterns *(continued)*

Project Description

The Ancient China Museum director is anxious to obtain a Chinese lantern for the museum collection. Make a replica of a paper lantern that is fitting for an important museum of antiquities.

Materials

white drawing paper or construction paper, 12 x 18 inches
paints, markers, or crayons
scissors, tape, stapler
decorations such as glitter, yarn, tassels, gold stickers, fancy
    paper, sequins

Chinese Lanterns *(continued)*

Directions

1. Choose designs and colors for your lantern that follow ancient Chinese motifs. One idea would be to include animals, plants, and scenes from nature, and to use the color red which is considered lucky and is commonly used on Chinese lanterns.

2. Draw your design horizontally on the paper.

3. Fold the decorated paper the long way.

4. Cut along the long side from the fold stopping two inches from the open end. Make cuts every two inches.

5. Open the folded paper and staple the twelve-inch sides together at the top and bottom.

6. Cut a strip of paper six inches long and one-half inch wide. Glue or staple this strip of paper across one end of the lantern for the handle.

7. Decorate the lantern with glitter, tassels, gold stickers, sequins, or other decorations.

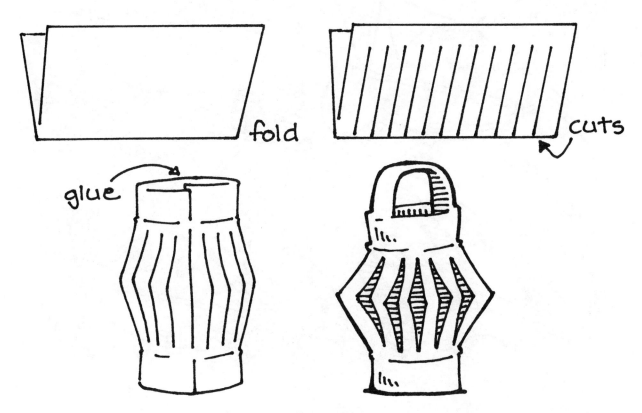

 Ancient China © 2006 The Learning Works

Ceremonial Kites

The Chinese probably invented kites about 3,000 years ago. The earliest kites were made of wood. When paper was invented, making kites became a pastime in which most people could partake. The kite developed into complex designs elaborately decorated and flown on religious and ceremonial occasions. Chinese emperors used kites to frighten the enemy in battle. They also used them to send signals to their troops in wartime. There were even kites large enough to carry warriors armed with bows and arrows that would fire down on the enemy below.

The designs on most Chinese kites have a symbolic meaning or are illustrations from Chinese folklore or history. Fish, insects, birds, tortoises, cranes, bats, butterflies, and dragons are popular designs. The complex shapes and designs are achieved by bending bamboo over a flame or soaking it in water. Over 100 pieces of shaped bamboo are used in the construction of some dragon head kites.

Ceremonial Kites *(continued)*

Project Description

The reputation of a brilliant kite designer has spread to the capital. Now the emperor requests that the kite maker design one worthy of being flown at an auspicious celebration. It must be beautiful and include traditional Chinese motifs in the design. Imagine what this kite must have looked like, and create a replica of it for your Ancient China Museum.

Materials

lightweight paper such as tracing paper
cardboard for cutting out reinforcing strips, dimensions
    should be as long as the kite edges
crepe paper streamers
tissue paper bows to be used with streamers
watercolors, marking pens, crayons
kite string
piece of 2 x 2 inch cardboard on which to wrap the string

Ancient China © 2006 The Learning Works

Ceremonial Kites *(continued)*

Directions

1. Design and cut out the shape of your kite. Kites with simple shapes are easier to make.

2. Plan the illustrations and then draw them on the kite.

3. Cut out cardboard strips to fit each side of the kite and glue them on the edges. Allow to dry thoroughly.

4. Cut out a cardboard strip to reinforce the middle of the kite. Tie one end of the kite string to the middle of this strip. Glue the reinforcing strip across the middle and allow to dry.

5. Glue or staple crepe paper streamers to the bottom end of the kite for a tail. Add crepe paper bows for a decorative touch.

6. Wrap the kite string onto the small cardboard square.

Chinese Fans

Fans were first used in China to keep off the dust raised by wheels of a cart or to fan away annoying pests. Gradually, fans acquired other uses. They became important for court performances, traditional Chinese operas, and other ceremonies. Artists and poets painted or wrote on them, and the rich and educated used them to show their social standing.

Fans were made out of many different materials including paper, silk, ivory, bamboo, wood, feathers, and various types of leaves.

Chinese Fans *(continued)*

Project Description

As you survey the Chinese fans in Beijing's premier ancient history museum, you realize immediately that one of them is particularly outstanding. It is a ceremonial fan made by an ancient artist known for painting traditional Chinese motifs. Make a copy of the fan to put in your own museum.

Materials

    card stock or poster board
    paints, marking pens, or watercolors
    scissors
    sticks such as a tongue depressor or craft sticks
    decorative paper

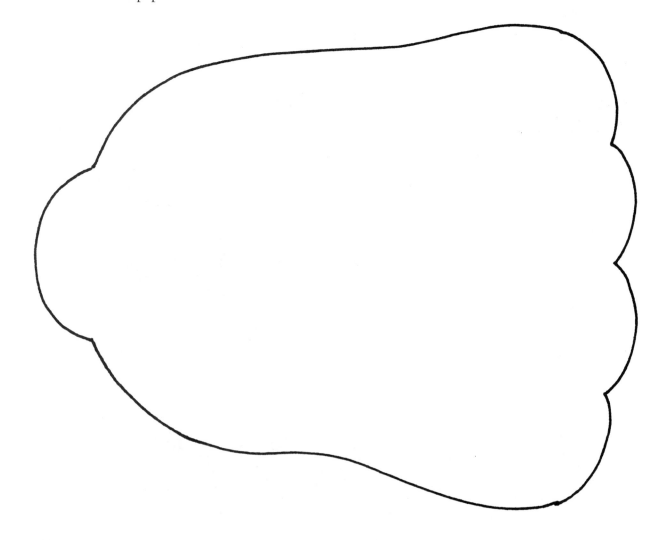

Chinese Fans *(continued)*

Directions

1. Draw the shape of a ceremonial fan on a piece of cardboard or poster board, or use the pattern on page 30.

2. Cut out the fan.

3. Use paints, marking pens, or watercolors to paint your design on the fan.

4. Paint a border around the edge of the fan to simulate wood or ivory, or glue on a border of decorative paper.

5. Decorate a stick and glue it to the back of the fan.

Ancient China © 2006 The Learning Works

Chinese Paper Cuts

For centuries paper cutting has been a popular Chinese craft. Cutouts were hung on doors to celebrate the new year and served as window coverings before glass windows came into use. Artists work with small scissors and thin red or black paper. They cut out unbelievably intricate pictures such as flowers, birds, trees, dragons, warriors, and wild stallions.

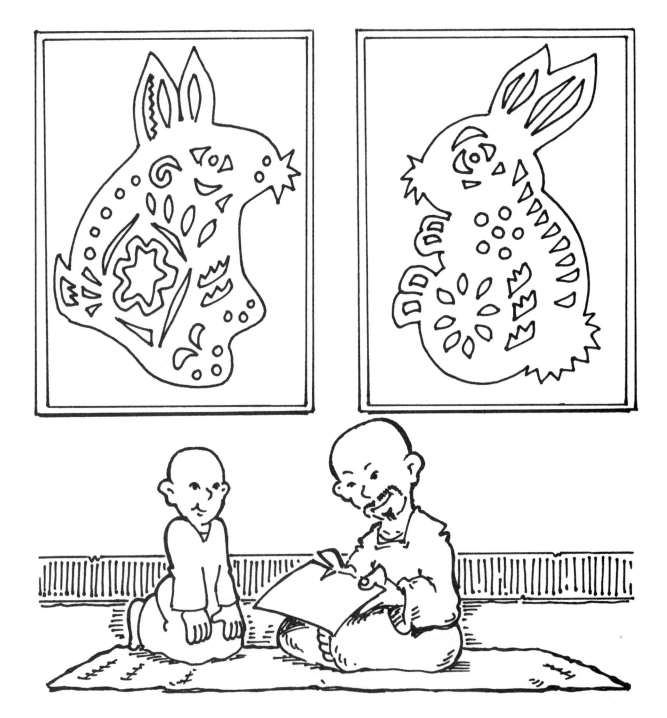

Chinese Paper Cuts *(continued)*

Project Description

The Chinese New Year is approaching and you want to decorate your museum with a series of traditional Chinese paper cuts. Design a paper cut, mount it, and display it in your museum.

Materials

red, black, or white construction paper, 9 x 12 inches
scissors
glue
pencil
patterns
a paper punch to help with difficult inside details

Ancient China © 2006 The Learning Works

Chinese Paper Cuts *(continued)*

Directions

1. Enlarge one of the designs in this section or create one of your own. Plan your paper cut with enough edges touching one another so the art will not fall apart when finished.

2. For symmetrical designs, fold the paper in half before tracing the pattern onto the paper, as shown.

3. If the design is not symmetrical, simply trace the pattern onto the paper.

4. Cut out the design. Use a paper punch to start cuts in difficult areas.

5. Carefully glue the design onto another piece of colored paper.

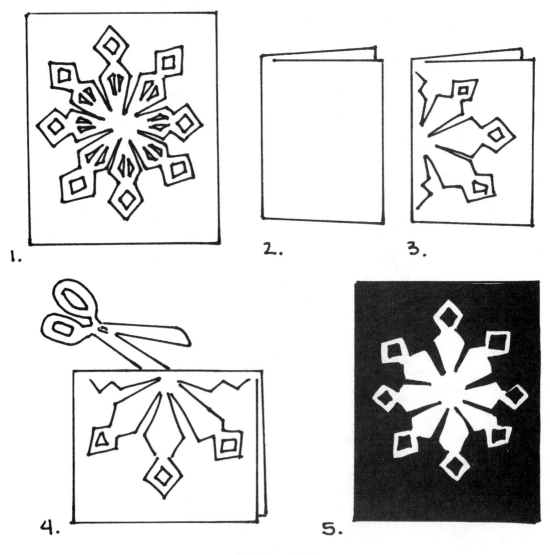

Ancient China © 2006 The Learning Works

Chinese Opera Masks

Opera is as popular in China as a baseball game might be in the United States. A Chinese opera brings together many elements to create a magnificent—sometimes rowdy—production. A typical opera might include songs, an orchestra with a large percussion section, dancing, acting, poetry, mime, acrobatics, elaborate costumes and headdresses, and unusual and dramatic masks. Every aspect of Chinese opera is highly symbolic. The audience can tell the actor's character by the color of makeup, body language, and pantomime.

Ancient China © 2006 The Learning Works

Chinese Opera Masks *(continued)*

Project Description

Your fame as a costume designer for the opera has spread throughout the kingdom. Recently, you were commissioned by the emperor to design a mask—an elaborate opera mask—for an important character in a new opera. You have been given the option of designing a papier mache mask for a loyal, courageous, and brave character; a cruel, brutal warrior; or a character of your choice. This must be your best work because, when the production is over, the mask will hang in the Ancient China Museum.

Color Symbolism for Opera Masks

Red: loyalty, courage
Purple: wisdom, bravery
Black: loyalty, integrity
White: cruelty, treachery
Blue: valor, resolution
Green: chivalry
Yellow: brutality
Gold and silver: supernatural characters
    such as demons and spirits

Ancient China © 2006 The Learning Works

Chinese Opera Masks *(continued)*

Materials

a large balloon, blown up, to use as a mold for the face
materials for papier mache
paper towels, brown paper bags, or other paper
glue
scissors
tempera or poster paints
masking tape
ribbons, sequins, yarn, glitter, and other decorative items

Ancient China © 2006 The Learning Works

Chinese Opera Masks *(continued)*

Directions

1. Blow up a balloon until it is big enough to simulate the size of a face.

2. Use the balloon as a mold for the mask.

3. Follow the directions for papier mache found on pages 21–22. Papier mache over half of the area of the balloon.

4. When the mask is thoroughly dry, pop the balloon and discard it.

5. Cut out the eyes with scissors or a sharp knife (adult supervision required).

6. Paint the mask. Use a variety of shapes and colors to represent traditional makeup.

7. Add hair, headdresses, beards, and other touches to create a traditional mask.

Royal Silk Robes

The clothes of rich and poor Chinese during the ancient dynasties were very different. Peasant farmers wore loose garments made of hemp, a rough fabric woven from plant fibers. Silk was reserved for the rich. Emperors chose the finest silk as the official fabric for their stately robes. Some of the most elaborate silk robes were made during the Qing Dynasty (1644–1912). The most famous were the dragon robes. Designs such as mountains, clouds, cranes, mandarin ducks, other animals, and plants were often used in the designs. They were decorated with symbols from traditional Chinese mythology. The color, cut, and symbolic decorations indicate the rank and status of the wearer. An emperor or empress were the only ones allowed to wear yellow robes bearing the five-toe dragon motif.

Ancient China © 2006 The Learning Works

Royal Silk Robes *(continued)*

Project Description

Imagine that you have been commissioned by the emperor to create an elaborate silk robe for an upcoming festival. It must be made from the finest silk and embellished with gold thread, peacock feathers, and pearls and embroidered with the finest of threads. And don't forget the dragon— a symbol of the emperor's power to mediate between heaven and earth. Create a smaller version of the imaginary silk robe on a piece of sheeting. Hang the finished robe in your Ancient China Museum.

Materials

    white sheet, about 2 x 3 feet (or use a poster board)
    fabric paints
    marking pens
    gold pens
    ribbons, sequins, beads, feathers, and other decorative things
    pieces of ornate fabrics, such as silk or brocade
    scissors
    large piece of heavy red or black paper (for mounting
        the robe)
    stapler

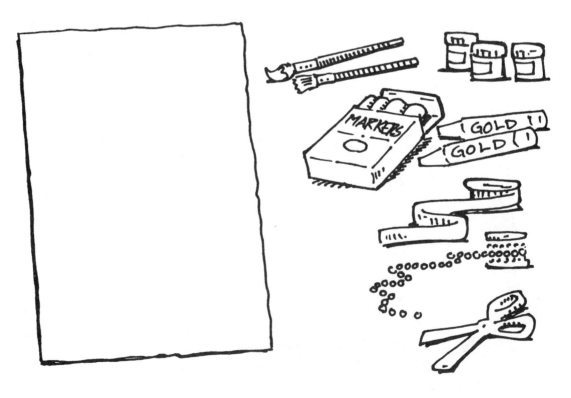

Royal Silk Robes *(continued)*

Directions

1. Make a sketch of the robe design on a piece of paper.

2. Use symbols that stand for the emperor's authority in your design. You might use designs such as multicolored lines, frothy ocean waves, colorful stringy clouds, animals, circles, or Chinese characters.

3. Cut out the sheet in the shape of the robe. Draw the design on the sheet with marking pens or fabric pens. Add decorative fabrics, ribbons, jewels, and other fancy items.

4. Use a stapler to mount the robe on a heavy piece of red or black paper.

5. Write a description of the robe and an explanation of the symbols incorporated into the design.

Ancient China © 2006 The Learning Works

Valley of the Ming Tombs

Of the sixteen emperors who ruled China during the Ming Dynasty (1368–1644 A.D.), thirteen are buried in elaborate complexes in the Valley of the Ming Tombs north of Beijing, China. Occupying a natural site, the tombs look down from their hillside locations onto the floor of the valley. A ceremonial road known as the Sacred Way snakes through the valley. The Sacred Way is four miles long and leads to the first restored Ming tomb. Deceased emperors were carried along the Sacred Way during the funeral ceremony. The Sacred Way is lined by twenty-four large stone animals—elephants, lions, mythological beasts—and stone figures of court and military officials.

Valley of the Ming Tombs (continued)

Project Description

The museum would like a team of designers to make a model of the Sacred Road leading to the tombs, the animals and warriors lining the Sacred Road, and several temples associated with the actual tombs of emperors. Work with a team of museum experts to create the model. You might want to include an actual funeral procession in your model.

Materials

aluminum foil
marking pens
masking tape
paint
cardboard
scissors
glue

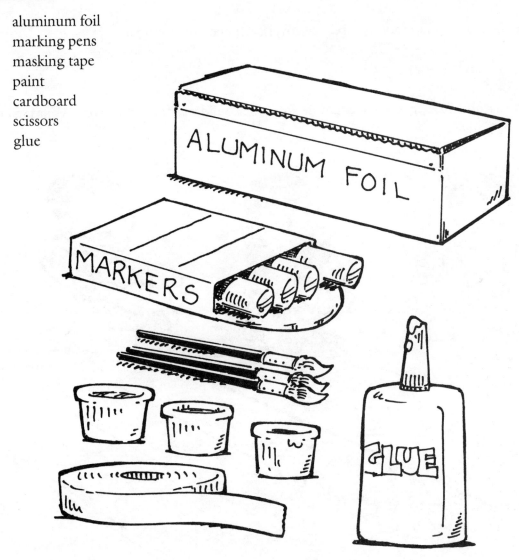

Valley of the Ming Tombs *(continued)*

Directions

1. On a sheet of paper, make a plan that details the components of the Valley of the Ming Tombs that you will include in your model.

2. Use foil to create the animals and warriors. Gently crumple foil together. If you squeeze too hard, the foil compresses and the person or animal gets too thin.

3. Use extra pieces of foil to strengthen arms and legs.

4. Take the masking tape and completely cover each person or animal.

5. Paint or draw in authentic details.

6. Using cardboard, construct the temple and other buildings that you have in your layout. Paint in details.

Ancient China © 2006 The Learning Works

Silk Road

Marco Polo traveled the Silk Road in the 1200s, but thousands of years before his time, a steady stream of traders, pilgrims, soldiers, adventurers, and refugees traveled back and forth along this same route. The Silk Road stretched for 7,000 miles as it connected oases and trading towns from China to the Mediterranean Sea. International trade thrived because caravans could travel with some sense of security. The cost of moving goods over such a long distance was high, so only items of great value were carried such as silk, bronzeware, ceramics, spices, tea, gems, linens, and glass.

CONSTANTINOPLE

Silk Road *(continued)*

Project Description

You are a trader making a trip to China to buy luxury items to be sold in your shop in Constantinople. Keep a journal of your journey explaining routes you took, descriptions of the sights and sounds, examples of transportation and dangers, and other people that you met along the way. You have no idea that your journal will be found 900 years later and placed in a museum of ancient Chinese antiquities.

Materials

a sheet of heavy paper, 9 x 12 inches, in tan, brown,
    or ivory for cover
white paper, 8½ x 11 inches, for inserts
pens, colored pencils
raffia
hole punch
tea bag
instant coffee grains

9" X 12" HEAVY PAPER

8½" X 11" WHITE PAPER

INSTANT COFFEE

Silk Road *(continued)*

Directions

1. To make the cover of your journal, fold a piece of heavy paper in half so it measures 6 x 9 inches.

2. To make the journal inserts, fold two or more pieces of 8½ x 11 inch paper in half.

3. Decorate the cover in a traditional Chinese design.

4. If you want to make your journal look old, color the paper by gently dabbing a tea bag soaked in hot water across the paper. Be careful not to tear the paper. To add brown age spots, sprinkle individual grains of instant coffee onto the damp paper. Age your journal before you bind it.

5. Punch two holes on the folded side of the cover, about one inch from the edge. Using these holes as a guide, punch two holes along the folded side of the insert sheets.

6. Insert the inside sheets into the cover and thread the raffia through the holes to bind your journal.

7. In your journal, record events that you experienced along the Silk Road. Include drawings of people, buildings, and geographical features that impressed you.

Ancient China © 2006 The Learning Works

Chinese Porcelain

Porcelain is a highly refined variety of ordinary pottery. The Chinese discovered the secret of manufacturing porcelain in the ninth century. The process produced a thin, almost translucent, piece of pottery that was whiter than other pottery types and better able to absorb colored dyes.

Graceful and beautiful blue and white porcelain is one of the most popular types. Blue and white designs included the lotus, human characters, flowers, fruit, dragons, phoenixes, birds, animals, and other patterns.

Porcelain became a valuable item for trade with Europeans. Great quantities of it were taken to Europe where it was called "china."

Ancient China © 2006 The Learning Works

Chinese Porcelain *(continued)*

Project Description

Imagine a family business so secretive that family members spy on one another for fear someone might reveal their secret formulas and techniques to rival companies. This was the way the highly competitive porcelain industry operated during the Song Dynasty (960–1279 A.D.). Pretend that you are a member of a highly respected family that makes porcelain. You have been asked to create a new pattern for the royal court. Make a papier mache model of a dish with your porcelain pattern painted on it. Display the dish in the Ancient China Museum.

Materials

> a dish to use as a mold
> petroleum jelly
> strips of paper towels
> paste
> blue and white tempera paint

Ancient China © 2006 The Learning Works

Chinese Porcelain *(continued)*

Directions

1. Put a thick layer of petroleum jelly over the outside and rim of the dish.

2. Follow the directions for papier mache on pages 21–22.

3. Cover the back of the bowl with 4 layers of paper strips. Place them crosswise over the preceding layer of strips.

4. Let your dish dry for 24 hours.

5. Remove the papier mache dish from the regular dish. Use a table knife to loosen it, if necessary.

6. Paint the papier mache dish white.

7. Create a blue and white porcelain design patterned after traditional Chinese designs.

8. Paint your design on the inside and outside of the papier mache dish with tempera paints.

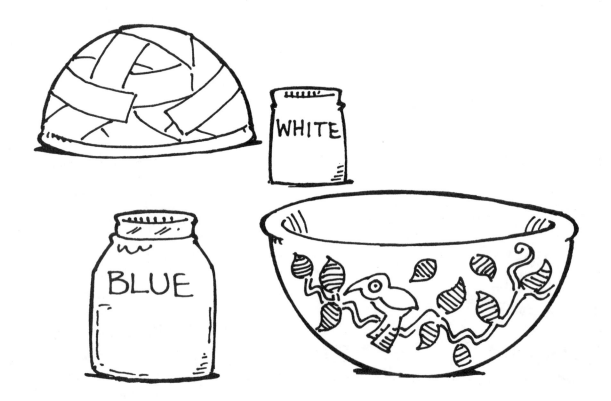

Ancient China © 2006 The Learning Works

Chinese Scrolls

The art of Chinese scroll painting dates back at least 4,000 years. The scroll designs include subjects such as animals, birds, flowers, people, landscapes, and simple calligraphy. Paintings and calligraphy were done on paper or silk and hung vertically or rolled horizontally. Many of the great Chinese scroll painters actually began as talented calligraphers. Using an ink-filled brush on silk or paper, calligraphers could express their innermost thoughts and feelings.

Chinese Scrolls *(continued)*

Project Description

Your reputation as a landscape artist and calligrapher is known throughout the Chinese empire. Every stroke you make is carefully placed; every part of the painting is carefully composed. Recently, an envoy brought you a directive from the emperor: Create a scroll that can be hung in the palace to honor the first day of Spring. You are honored and begin working on the painting that, hundreds of years from now, will be hanging in a museum of Chinese antiquities.

Materials

large pieces of white construction paper glued together to
    create a scroll approximately 22 x 48 inches
black watercolor paint or drawing ink
gold paint
watercolor paint brushes
decorative patterned wallpaper or construction paper
yarn or ribbon
thin wooden dowels
glue

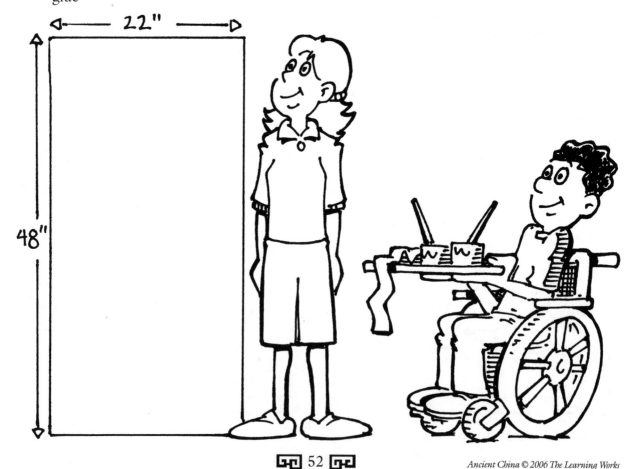

Ancient China © 2006 The Learning Works

Chinese Scrolls *(continued)*

Directions

1. Glue paper together to create a scroll approximately 22 inches wide and 48 inches long.

2. Plan the painting you will make for the scroll. The composition of a hanging scroll usually places the foreground at the bottom of the scroll with the middle and distant objects moving up toward the top of the scroll.

3. Paint your landscape on the scroll. Use different gradations of black paint. Add gold paint highlights if appropriate.

4. Research Chinese characters that express the beauty or meaning behind your painting. Paint several of the Chinese characters vertically onto the scroll.

5. Glue one strip of wallpaper or construction paper on the top and one strip on the bottom of the scroll.

6. Glue the top and bottom of the scroll to thin wooden dowels.

7. Attach a length of ribbon or yarn to the ends of the top dowel to hang the scroll.

 Ancient China © 2006 The Learning Works

Chinese Proverbs

Proverbs are popular sayings which contain advice or state a generally accepted truth. They function as "folk wisdom," general advice about how to act and live. Confucius (551–479 B.C.) was known for his sayings or proverbs. He was probably the most important contributor to the religious philosophy of China. Following his death, his followers spread his ideas and collected his teachings into a group of books called the Five Classics.

Confucius is credited with these sayings:

"A journey of a thousand miles begins with a single step."

"Our greatest glory is not in never falling, but in rising every time we fall."

"To know what is right and not do it is the worst cowardice."

"It is not possible for one to teach others who cannot teach his own family."

"The superior man is modest in his speech but exceeds in his actions."

"To be able under all circumstances to practice five things constitutes perfect virtue; these five things are gravity, generosity of soul, sincerity, earnestness, and kindness."

"If you enjoy what you do, you'll never work another day in your life."

"What you do not want others to do to you, do not do to others."

"A man who has made a mistake and doesn't correct it is committing another mistake."

Chinese Proverbs *(continued)*

Project Description

The director of the museum would like to recognize the contributions of Confucius to Chinese culture, and suggests that you choose one of Confucius' sayings and create a greeting card to use for museum correspondence.

Materials

several pieces of high quality paper, 5½ x 8½ inches each
black ink
marking pens or paints
decorative paper
glue

Ancient China © 2006 The Learning Works

Chinese Proverbs *(continued)*

Directions

1. Fold a piece of paper in half to create a card, approximately 4¼ x 5½ inches.

2. Choose one of the sayings on the preceding page, or find another saying from Confucius.

3. Think about the meaning of the saying and plan ways to illustrate it.

4. Use black ink, paint, or marking pens to draw the illustration on the front of the card.

5. After the illustration has dried, write Confucius' saying on either the front or the inside of the card.

6. Decorate the card by gluing narrow strips of fancy paper at the top or bottom of the card.

Ancient China © 2006 The Learning Works

The Zodiac

China uses the Buddhist system of organizing time into twelve-year cycles. Each year comes under the special protection of an animal. A legend explains that all the animals of the world were invited to come and pay a last visit to the Buddha before he died. Only twelve animals came—the rat, ox, tiger, rabbit, dragon, snake, horse, ram (sheep), monkey, rooster, dog, and boar (pig). In order to reward the animals for their loyalty, the Buddha named a year after each. A complete calendar cycle is 60 years, which includes the twelve-year cycle being repeated five times.

Ancient China © 2006 The Learning Works

The Zodiac *(continued)*

Project Description

It is nearly the beginning of a new year and the empress is anxious for her yearly zodiac calendar. Pretend you are a famous Chinese astronomer known for your elaborate calendars. Create a calendar in a fashion you deem worthy of the empress and worthy of being displayed in an ancient China museum.

Materials

    a large piece of heavy paper
    zodiac animal pictures, or your own drawings
    zodiac birth year chart for reference
    compass
    scissors
    Chinese motifs such as clouds, fire, bats, pearl, cloud border,
        still water border, sea waves, sea spray
    gold foil and other decorative papers

Ancient China © 2006 The Learning Works

The Zodiac *(continued)*

Directions

1. Draw a large circle on the heavy paper and cut it out.

2. Divide this circular piece of paper into twelve wedges. A compass does this easily.

3. Draw the animals and various other elements of the zodiac on separate sheets of colored paper. This method will create more contrast and prevent the calendar being ruined by a mistake. Draw the animals in a Chinese style, not necessarily realistically.

4. Glue the animals and other elements onto the large circle. Place one animal on each wedge. Follow the order of the twelve-year cycle: rat, ox, tiger, rabbit, dragon, snake, horse, ram, monkey, rooster, dog, and boar (pig).

5. Be sure to include traditional Chinese motifs on the borders and remember that red is a favorite color. Add gold highlights and other decorative papers to make the calendar elaborate.

An Ancient Pagoda

The pagoda—a type of tower associated with Buddhist temples—originated in India and then spread throughout Asia as Buddhism spread eastward. Pagodas have many stories, usually from three to fifteen, which are stacked one on top of another and decrease in size from bottom to top. The highest pagodas are considered the most sacred. Each story has an overhanging roof that curves up at the edges and is elaborately decorated with tiles, bright paint, and carvings.

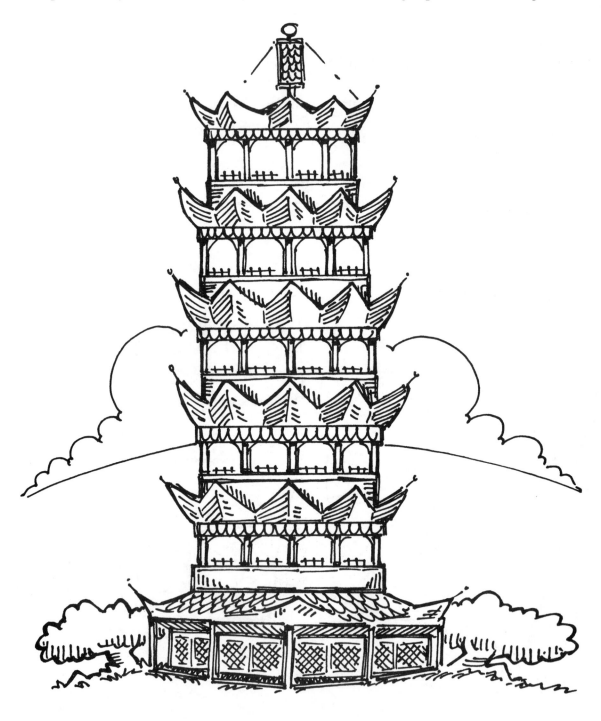

An Ancient Pagoda *(continued)*

Project Description

You have been directed by the museum director to add architectural elements as backdrops to the displays in the museum. Create an original pagoda with overhanging roofs, elaborate tiles, intricate carvings, and bright colors. On the museum card, explain your unique design and tell why it is an architectural wonder.

Materials

poster board
tempera, poster paints, or marking pens
colored construction paper
foil, decorative papers
glue
foam sheets in various patterns are available in craft stores,
    but are optional

An Ancient Pagoda *(continued)*

Directions

1. Draw your pagoda outline on a piece of poster board.

2. Use paint or marking pens to add traditional details to the pagoda.

3. Glue on decorative items to create three-dimensional tiles, carvings, overhanging roofs, and other architectural effects.

Historical Banners

Banners look like flags but are usually hung from a crosspiece or frame. Historically, banners were used by rulers or military commanders, but they can be used to symbolize local or state government, religious beliefs, family history, or school, community, and national events.

Ancient China © 2006 The Learning Works

Historical Banners *(continued)*

Project Description

Design a banner that commemorates the opening of your Ancient China Museum. It should include elements that symbolize museums, the importance of learning, and cultural diversity. Other design suggestions are to include aspects of ancient Chinese history and culture and typical Chinese motifs.

Materials

posterboard, paper, muslin, or felt: one large piece for the
    backing of the banner
scraps of paper, felt, fabric, yarn, and other decorative items
    for the designs on the banner
glue
scissors
crayons, paint, marking pens, or fabric pens
a dowel which extends one or two inches beyond the edges
    of the banner
cording or yarn

Directions

1. Plan the design and shape of the banner on a separate piece of paper.

2. Cut out the banner from the large piece of poster board, felt, or muslin.

3. Glue on pieces of paper, felt, fabric, yarn, or other decorative items to complete the design of the banner.

4. Glue the top of the banner to the dowel. Let the glue dry thoroughly.

5. Add yarn or cording to the ends of the dowel to create a way to hang it from the ceiling or on a wall.